This book belongs to

....

Copyright © 2016

make believe ideas ltd

The Wilderness, Berkhamsted, Hertfordshire, HP4 2AZ, UK.
501 Nelson Place, P.O. Box 141000, Nashville, TN 37214-1000, USA.

www.makebelieveideas.com

A PRANK STAR READER

PRANK
star

Illustrated by Stuart Lynch

make
believe
ideas

Reading together

This *book* is an ideal first reader for your child, combining simple jokes with entertaining illustrations.

Here are some of the many ways you can help your child with early steps in reading.

Encourage your child to:

- Look at and explore the detail in the pictures.
- Sound out the letters in each word.
- Read and repeat each short sentence.

Look at the pictures

Make the most of each page by talking about the pictures and pointing out key words.

Here are some questions you can use to discuss each page as you go along:

- Do you like this picture?
- What are the characters doing?
- What is funny about this picture?

Test understanding

It is one thing to understand the meaning of individual words, but you want to make sure that your child understands the text.

- Play "find the mistake." Read the text as your child looks at the words with you, but make an obvious mistake to see if he or she has understood. Ask your child to correct you and provide the right word.

- After reading the text, close the book and make up questions to ask your child.

Prank Star quiz

At the end of the book, there is a simple quiz. Ask your child to read the jokes and pair them up with their punch lines.

Key words

These pages provide practice with very common words used in the context of the book. Read the sentences with your child and encourage him or her to make up more sentences using the key words listed around the border.

Picture dictionary

Use the picture dictionary to examine the spellings of some of the words in this book and then get your child to try writing them on his or her own.

What did the ocean say to the lifeguard?

Nothing, it just waved!

How do you make
a toilet roll?

What's orange
and sounds like
a parrot?

When is the
best time to visit
the dentist?

13

What do frogs
like for lunch?

14

How do you make
a milk shake?

Tell it a scary story!

What's black and white and goes up and down?

19

Why was the spaghetti sent to bed?

What's a pirate's favorite letter?

22

Why did the snake go to school?

What do you say when you meet a three-headed alien?

Prank Star quiz

Can you pair up the jokes and the punch lines?

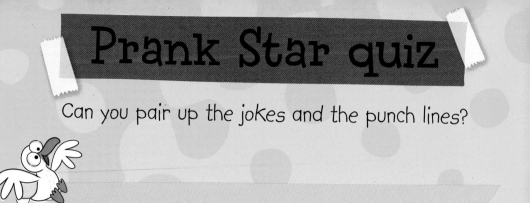

What did the ocean say to the lifeguard?

What do frogs like for lunch?

How do you make a milk shake?

What's a pirate's favorite letter?

The Greeksss

JULIUS CAESSSAR

Why did the snake go to school?

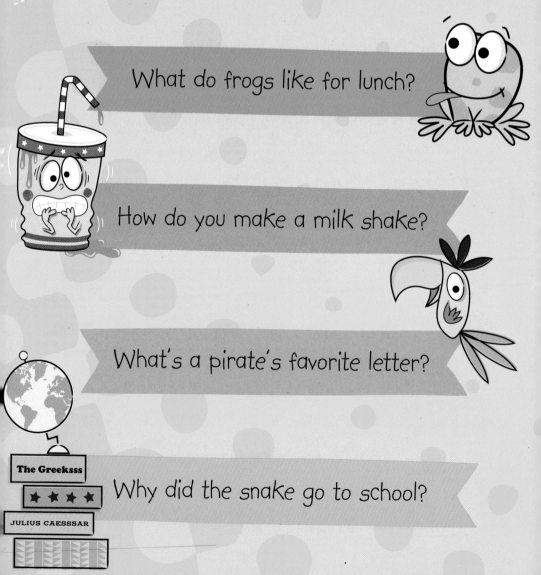

Key words

Here are some key words used in context.
Help your child to use other words from
the border in simple sentences.

Frogs **like** flies.

The milk shake **is** scared.

The ocean waves **at** the lifeguard.

The penguin jumps **on** a trampoline.

Pirates like **the** letter R.

The spaghetti goes **to** bed.

Picture dictionary

dentist

flies

frog

lifeguard

milk shake

pasta

penguin

pirate

snake